"It's hard to connect with your child without first understanding where they are. As counselors and speakers at parenting events across the country, we spend a great deal of time teaching parents about development. To know *where* your child is—not just physically, but emotionally, socially, and spiritually, helps you to truly know and understand *who* your child is. And that understanding is the key to connecting. The Phase Guides give you the tools to do just that. Our wise friends Reggie and Kristen have put together an insightful, hopeful, practical, and literal year-by-year guide that will help you to understand and connect with your child at every age."

SISSY GOFF
M.ED., LPC-MHSP, DIRECTOR OF CHILD & ADOLESCENT COUNSELING AT DAYSTAR COUNSELING MINISTRIES IN NASHVILLE, TENNESSEE, SPEAKER AND AUTHOR OF ARE MY KIDS ON TRACK?

"These resources for parents are fantastically empowering, absolute in their simplicity, and completely doable in every way. The hard work that has gone into the Phase Project will echo through the next generation of children in powerful ways."

JENNIFER WALKER
RN BSN, AUTHOR AND FOUNDER OF MOMS ON CALL

"We all know where we want to end up in our parenting, but how to get there can seem like an unsolved mystery. Through the Phase Project series, Reggie Joiner and Kristen Ivy team up to help us out. The result is a resource that guides us through the different seasons of raising children, and provides a road map to parenting in such a way that we finish up with very few regrets."

SANDRA STANLEY
FOSTER CARE ADVOCATE, BLOGGER, WIFE TO ANDY STANLEY, MOTHER OF THREE

"Not only are the Phase Guides the most creative and well-thought-out guides to parenting I have ever encountered, these books are ESSENTIAL to my daily parenting. With a 13-year-old, 11-year-old, and 9-year-old at home I am swimming in their wake of daily drama and delicacy. Th_____ _____ ꞌinder to enjoy every second. Because it's just

CARLOS WHITTAKER
AUTHOR, SPEAKER, FATHER OF THREE

"As the founder of Minnie's Food Pantry, _____ month with children who will benefit from _____, and nuggets of information on how to celebrate and understand the phases of their child's life. Too often we feel like we're losing our mind when sweet little Johnny starts to change his behavior into a person we do not know. I can't wait to start implementing the principles of these books with my clients to remind them . . . it's just a phase."

CHERYL JACKSON
FOUNDER OF MINNIE'S FOOD PANTRY, AWARD-WINNING PHILANTHROPIST, AND GRANDMOTHER

"I began exploring this resource with my counselor hat on, thinking how valuable this will be for the many parents I spend time with in my office. I ended up taking my counselor hat off and putting on my parent hat. Then I kept thinking about friends who are teachers, coaches, youth pastors, and children's ministers, who would want this in their hands. What a valuable resource the Orange team has given us to better understand and care for the kids and adolescents we love. I look forward to sharing it broadly."

DAVID THOMAS
LMSW, DIRECTOR OF FAMILY COUNSELING, DAYSTAR COUNSELING MINISTRIES, SPEAKER AND AUTHOR OF ARE MY KIDS ON TRACK? *AND* WILD THINGS: THE ART OF NURTURING BOYS

"I have always wished someone would hand me a manual for parenting. Well, the Phase Guides are more than what I wished for. They guide, inspire, and challenge me as a parent—while giving me incredible insight into my children at each age and phase. Our family will be using these every year!"

COURTNEY DEFEO
AUTHOR OF IN THIS HOUSE, WE WILL GIGGLE, *MOTHER OF TWO*

"As I speak to high school students and their parents, I always wonder to myself: What would it have been like if they had better seen what was coming next? What if they had a guide that would tell them what to expect and how to be ready? What if they could anticipate what is predictable about the high school years before they actually hit? These Phase Guides give a parent that kind of preparation so they can have a plan when they need it most."

JOSH SHIPP
AUTHOR, TEEN EXPERT, AND YOUTH SPEAKER

"The Phase Guides are incredibly creative, well researched, and filled with inspirational actions for everyday life. Each age-specific guide is catalytic for equipping parents to lead and love their kids as they grow up. I'm blown away and deeply encouraged by the content and by its creators. I highly recommend Phase resources for all parents, teachers, and influencers of children. This is the stuff that challenges us and changes our world. Get them. Read them. And use them!"

DANIELLE STRICKLAND
OFFICER WITH THE SALVATION ARMY, AUTHOR, SPEAKER, MOTHER OF TWO

"It's true that parenting is one of life's greatest joys but it is not without its challenges. If we're honest, parenting can sometimes feel like trying to choreograph a dance to an ever-changing beat. It can be clumsy and riddled with well-meaning missteps. If parenting is a dance, this Parenting Guide is a skilled instructor refining your technique and helping you move gracefully to a steady beat. For those of us who love to plan ahead, this guide will help you anticipate what's to come so you can be poised and ready to embrace the moments you want to enjoy."

TINA NAIDOO
MSSW, LCSW EXECUTIVE DIRECTOR, THE POTTER'S HOUSE OF DALLAS, INC.

PARENTING YOUR SEVENTH GRADER

A GUIDE TO MAKING THE MOST OF THE "WHO'S GOING?" PHASE

KRISTEN IVY AND REGGIE JOINER

PARENTING YOUR SEVENTH GRADER
A GUIDE TO MAKING THE MOST OF THE
"WHO'S GOING?" PHASE

Published by Orange, a division of The reThink Group, Inc.,
5870 Charlotte Lane, Suite 300,
Cumming, GA 30040 U.S.A.

All Scripture quotations, unless otherwise indicated, are taken from the Holy
Bible, New International Version®, NIV®. Copyright ©1973, 1978, 1984, 2011 by
Biblica, Inc.™ Used by permission of Zondervan. All rights reserved worldwide.
www.zondervan.com The "NIV" and "New International Version" are trademarks
registered in the United States Patent and Trademark Office by Biblica, Inc.™

©2017 The Phase Project
Authors: Kristen Ivy and Reggie Joiner
Lead Editor: Karen Wilson
Editing Team: Melanie Williams, Hannah Crosby, Sherry Surratt

Art Direction: Ryan Boon and Hannah Crosby
Book Design: FiveStone and Sharon van Rossum
Project Manager : Nate Brandt

Printed in the United States of America
First Edition 2017
6 7 8 9 10 11 12 13 14 15

08/20/2018

Special thanks to:

*Jim Burns, Ph.D for guidance and consultation
on having conversations about sexual integrity*

*Jon Acuff for guidance and consultation on having
conversations about technological responsibility*

*Jean Sumner, MD for guidance and consultation
on having conversations about healthy habits*

*Every educator, counselor, community leader, and
researcher who invested in the Phase Project*

TABLE OF CONTENTS

HOW TO USE THIS ~~BOOK~~ ~~JOURNAL~~ GUIDE

The guide you hold in your hand doesn't have very many words, but it does have a lot of ideas. Some of these ideas come from thousands of hours of research. Others come from parents, educators, and volunteers who spend every day with kids the same age as yours. This guide won't tell you everything about your kid, but it will tell you a few things about kids at this age.

The best way to use this guide is to take what these pages tell you about seventh graders and combine it with what you know is true about *your* seventh grader.

Let's sum it up:

THINGS ABOUT SEVENTH GRADERS +
THOUGHTS ABOUT *YOUR* SEVENTH GRADER =
YOUR GUIDE TO THE NEXT 52 WEEKS OF PARENTING

After each idea in this guide, there are pages with a few questions designed to prompt you to think about your kid, your family, and yourself as a parent. The only guarantee we give to parents who use this guide is this: You will mess up some things as a parent this year. Actually, that's a guarantee to every parent, regardless. But you, you picked up this book! You want to be a better parent. And that's what we hope this guide will do: help you parent your seventh grader just a little better, simply because you paused to consider a few ideas that can help you make the most of this phase.

THE SEVENTH GRADE PHASE

"Wow . . . really?"
"God bless you!"
"I'll pray for you!"

These are the top three responses I get from people when they learn I work with middle school students for a living. And usually, it's said in a tone of confusion or skepticism. Most adults simply can't believe someone would choose my profession on purpose.

When you tell someone you're parenting a seventh grader, you probably get these responses as well. And for good reason. Parenting a seventh grader is hard work! For most of us, the days of sweet cuddles and handmade gifts are fading into the background.

In their place, we're confronted with a kid who is constantly changing from week to week, day to day, even hour to hour. One day you might come home and they meet you like a puppy! Their hopeful expression suggests, "I'm so glad you're here! Can you play with me?" Then, the very next day, they've turned into a skittish cat, only appearing long enough to give you a glance, a hiss, and turn their tails at you as they walk up to their room.

These developmentally schizophrenic creatures are challenging. Just when you think you have them figured out, they turn on you. They're expensive, frustrating, uncomfortably honest, and many times, they just smell bad. But if you look beyond the surface, you'll find that some of the most important, incredible, and God-ordained changes are happening in your seventh grader.

Their minds are changing faster than at any other time in life except the first few months after birth. Often the inconsistencies you experience from your seventh grader are just an expression of the inconsistency they feel as they oscillate between the joys of learning a new skill and the frustration of having no idea how to operate their new brain.

Their relationships are changing. They're surrounded by friends who are all navigating the same developmental changes they are. Take a moment to think about how complicated that is. You think you're frustrated by the dynamic personality of just one seventh grader? Try attempting to figure out your best friend whose brain is doing somersaults while your brain is doing the same thing!

When you understand what's going on inside your seventh grader, you may discover your frustration turning into fascination. Who else can approach life with the trust of a child and the logic of an adult?

Every once in a while, I run into someone who really gets seventh graders. Someone who understands not only why I do what I do, but why I love what I do. When I find someone who gets it, they say (with a smile and not a hint of sarcasm):

"That sounds fun!"
"What an important job!"
"I'll pray for you!"

And those are the same things I say to anyone who is parenting a seventh grader.

- TOM SHEFCHUNAS
MULTI-CAMPUS DIRECTOR OF MIDDLE SCHOOL FOR NORTHPOINT MINISTRIES

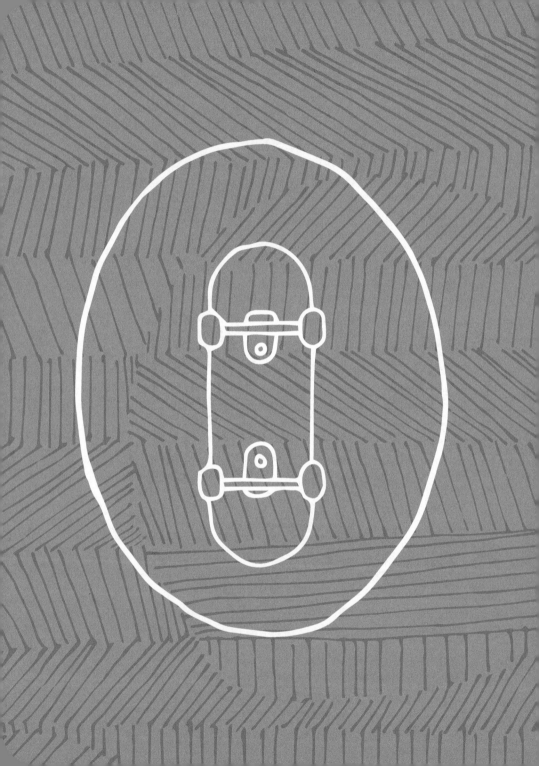

52
WEEKS
—
TO PARENT YOUR
SEVENTH GRADE

WHEN YOU SEE
HOW MUCH

Time

YOU HAVE LEFT

—

YOU TEND TO DO

More

WITH THE TIME
YOU HAVE NOW.

THERE ARE APPROXIMATELY

936 WEEKS

FROM THE TIME A BABY IS BORN
UNTIL THEY GROW UP AND MOVE TO
WHATEVER IS NEXT.

On the day your child starts seventh grade, you only have 312 weeks remaining. (You've already invested two thirds of your weeks.) You may feel as if you can watch time moving—simply by how quickly your middle schooler is growing and changing before your eyes. Time is moving more quickly now, and your kid is growing up—*fast*.

Every week counts. Of course, each week might not feel significant. There may be weeks this year when all you feel like you accomplished was logging thousands of miles driving your middle schooler where they need to go. That's okay.

Take a deep breath.
You don't have to get everything done this week.

But what happens in your child's life week after week, year after year, adds up. So, it's a good idea to put a number to your weeks.

MEASURE IT OUT.

Write down the number of weeks that have already passed since your seventh grader was born. Then write down the number of weeks you have left before they potentially graduate high school.

 HINT: If you want a little help counting it out, you can download the free Parent Cue app on all mobile platforms.

_____

_____

_____

CREATE A VISUAL COUNTDOWN.

Find a jar and fill it with one marble for each week you have remaining with your seventh grader. Then remove one marble every week as a reminder to make the most of your time.

Where can you place your visual countdown so you will see it frequently?

_____

_____

_____

_____

_____

Which day of the week is best for you to remove a marble?

_____

_____

_____

Is there anything you want to do each week as you remove a marble? _(Examples: say a prayer, write your kid a note, retell one favorite memory from this past week)_

_____

_____

_____

_____

_____

_____

_____

_____

_____

_____

_____

_____

_____

EVERY PHASE IS A

TIMEFRAME

IN A KID'S LIFE

WHEN YOU CAN

LEVERAGE

DISTINCTIVE

OPPORTUNITIES

TO INFLUENCE

THEIR

future.

YOU ONLY HAVE
52 WEEKS
WITH YOUR SEVENTH GRADER

while they are still in seventh grade.

Then they will be in eighth grade,

and you will never know them as a seventh grader again.

Or, to say it another way:

Before you know it, your kid will . . .

ask to go to the mall without you.

ask to go to the football game without you.

ask to go on a date (definitely, without you).

The point is this: The phase you are in now has remarkable potential. Before the end of seventh grade, there are some distinctive opportunities you don't want to miss. So, as you count down the next 52 weeks, pay attention to what makes these weeks uniquely different from the time you've already spent together and the weeks you will have when they move on to the next phase.

What are some things you have noticed about your seventh grader in this phase that you really enjoy?

_____

_____

_____

_____

_____

_____

_____

_____

_____

_____

_____

_____

_____

_____

_____

_____

_____

What is something new you are learning as a parent during this phase?

_____

_____

_____

_____

_____

_____

_____

_____

_____

_____

_____

_____

_____

_____

_____

_____

_____

_____

SEVENTH GRADE

—

THE PHASE WHEN
NOTHING YOU DO IS
COOL, WHAT THEY FEEL
RIGHT NOW MATTERS
MOST, AND ONE
SUDDENLY SOCIAL KID
WANTS TO KNOW,

"Who's going?"

NOW—YOU'RE EMBARRASSING.

Figuring out the new rules for your social behavior can be intimidating. When is it acceptable to walk over and say hello? Why do all your comments elicit an eye roll? Don't be caught off guard—you're transitioning to parenting an adolescent. This may be an awkward phase for you.

NOW—EVERYTHING HAPPENS IN A CROWD.

It may be hard to recognize your seventh grader amid all the other seventh graders. They walk the hall in pairs. They go to the mall in a herd. They build unfathomably large social media platforms. In seventh grade, the best place to be is wherever "everyone" goes.

NOW—IS REALLY ALL THAT MATTERS.

It's not that what you said this morning doesn't matter, it's just that they don't remember it. And it's not that they don't care about their future, it's just that the present is so much closer. Most seventh graders are hyperaware of their present reality. That means there isn't anything quite so motivating as *right now*. Look for ways to use *right now* to your advantage, and appeal to their present circumstances.

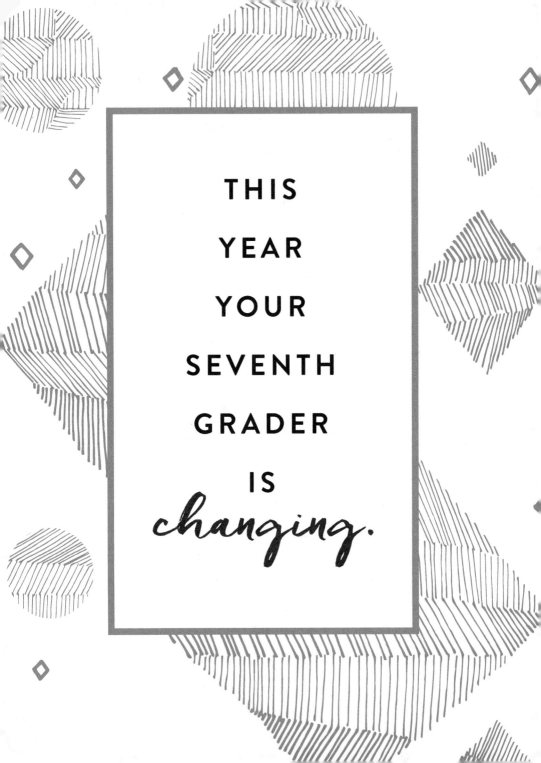

THIS
YEAR
YOUR
SEVENTH
GRADER
IS
changing.

PHYSICALLY

- Needs 9-11 hours of sleep each night and may easily fatigue or develop headaches

- Girls outpace guys in development

- Guys experience changes in height and body shape, and may develop body odor, body hair, and increased muscle mass

- Girls may develop body odor, body hair, and breasts; and menstruation is likely (10-16 years)

MENTALLY

- Able to see two sides of an argument

- Enjoys forming and sharing their opinion

- Solves multi-step, complex problems

- Has a hard time with organization and time management

- Sudden brain growth may lead to forgetfulness

SOCIALLY

- Often characterized as happy, silly, and loud

- May change friends to reflect new interests

- Interested in pop culture and new slang

- Needs non-parental adult influences

- Places a significant emphasis on peer opinions

- Girls (in particular) frequently display excessive meanness, increased attention to self-image, and a lack of confidence

EMOTIONALLY

- Enjoys silly and sometimes crude humor

- Benefits from talking about what they are feeling and why

- May be restless and need physical activity

- Tends to overschedule their time

What are some changes you are noticing in your seventh grader?

_____

_____

_____

_____

_____

_____

_____

You may disagree with some of the characteristics we've shared about seventh graders. That's because every seventh grader is unique. What makes your seventh grader different from seventh graders in general?

_____

_____

_____

_____

_____

_____

_____

_____

What impresses you about your seventh grader?

Mark this page. Some weeks it may be easy to focus only on what your seventh grader does wrong, so try to catch them doing something right. Write it down here. If you want to be really thorough, there are about 52 blank lines.

_____

_____

_____

_____

_____

_____

_____

_____

_____

_____

_____

_____

_____

_____

_____

_____

_____

_____

_____

_____

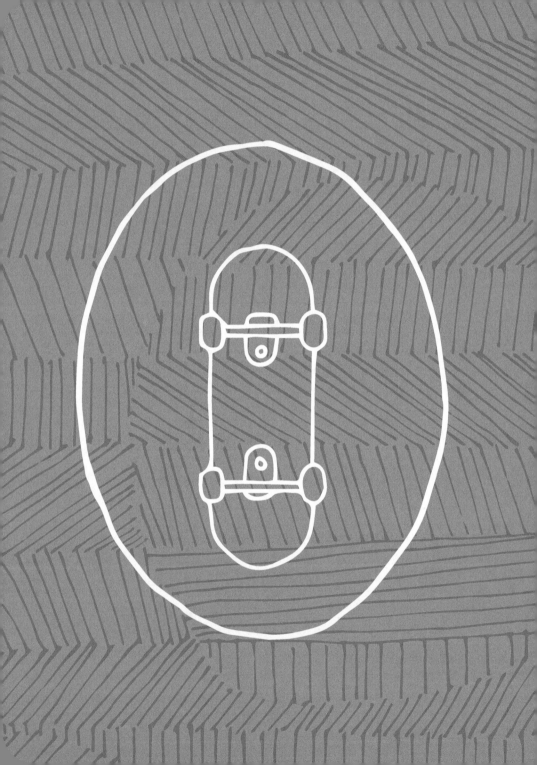

SIX THINGS

EVERY KID NEEDS

YOUR KID NEEDS 6 THINGS OVER TIME

LOVE
WORDS
WORK
TRIBES
STORIES
FUN

OVER THE NEXT 312 WEEKS, YOUR SEVENTH GRADER WILL NEED MANY THINGS:

Some of the things your kid needs will change from phase to phase, but there are six things every kid needs at every phase. In fact, these things may be the most important things you give your kid.

EVERY KID, AT EVERY PHASE, NEEDS . . .

LOVE
to give them a
sense of WORTH.

STORIES
to give them a bigger
PERSPECTIVE.

WORK
to give them
SIGNIFICANCE.

FUN
to give them
CONNECTION.

TRIBES
to give them
BELONGING.

WORDS
to give them
DIRECTION.

The next few pages are designed to help you think about how you will give your child these six things, right now—while they are in seventh grade.

EVERY KID

NEEDS

love

OVER TIME

—

TO GIVE THEM

A SENSE OF

worth.

ONE QUESTION YOUR SEVENTH GRADER IS ASKING

Your seventh grader is in a season of personal discovery. Not everyone makes the team. Interests and abilities change. Long-accepted values can come into question. On top of all that, this phase is a time of heightened self-awareness.

Your seventh grader is asking one major question:

"WHO AM I?"

Seventh graders realize no one is exactly like them—which can be both exhilarating and unnerving. This silent question gives insight into why seventh graders are often inconsistent in their friendships, behaviors, or style. As you parent your seventh grader, you have an opportunity to build their sense of worth when you do one thing:

AFFIRM their personal journey.

When you affirm their personal journey, you communicate . . .
"You are wonderfully and uniquely made,"
"Your perspective is important,"
and "I will love you no matter what."

In order to affirm your seventh grader, you need time together. What are some times during your week when you connect best? (Examples: the commute to school, eating a meal together, driving their friends, family game or movie night)

_____

_____

_____

_____

_____

_____

_____

_____

_____

_____

_____

_____

_____

_____

_____

_____

_____

Affirming your seventh grader requires paying attention to what they like. What does your seventh grader seem to enjoy the most right now? *(If you don't know, it's okay to ask them.)*

_____

_____

_____

_____

_____

_____

_____

_____

_____

_____

_____

_____

_____

_____

_____

_____

_____

_____

How might you try to rediscover what they like—even though it's changing often?

_____

_____

_____

_____

_____

_____

_____

_____

_____

_____

_____

_____

_____

_____

_____

_____

_____

_____

_____

It's impossible to consistently love someone as challenging as your seventh grader unless you have a little time for yourself. What can you do to refuel each week so you are able to give your seventh grader the love they need?

EVERY KID

NEEDS

stories

OVER TIME

—

TO GIVE THEM

A BIGGER

perspective.

BOOKS TO READ
WITH YOUR SEVENTH GRADER .

**THE TRUE CONFESSIONS
OF CHARLOTTE DOYLE**
by Avi

**AL CAPONE DOES MY
SHIRTS (SERIES)**
by Gennifer Choldenko

OUT OF MY MIND
by Sharon Draper

PRINCESS ACADEMY (SERIES)
by Shannon Hale

THE OUTSIDERS
by S.E. Hinton

THE THING ABOUT LUCK
by Cynthia Kadohata

**AN AMERICAN PLAGUE:
THE TRUE AND TERRIFYING
STORY OF THE YELLOW FEVER
EPIDEMIC OF 1793**
by Jim Murphy

ERAGON (SERIES)
by Christopher Paolini

JACOB HAVE I LOVED
by Katherine Paterson

A DAY NO PIGS WOULD DIE
by Robert Newton Peck

**THE SECRETS OF THE IMMORTAL
NICHOLAS FLAMEL (SERIES)**
by Michael Scott

**THE SNEECHES & YURTLE
THE TURTLE**
by Dr. Seuss

THE WITCH OF BLACKBIRD POND
by Elizabeth George Speare

MANIAC MAGEE
by Jerry Spinelli

STARGIRL
by Jerry Spinelli

TREASURE ISLAND
by Robert Louis Stevenson

GULLIVER'S TRAVELS
by Jonathan Swift

THE HOBBIT
by J.R.R. Tolkien

LOCOMOTION
by Jacqueline Woodson

Share a story. Whether it's a book, play, TV series, or movie, what are some stories that engage your seventh grader?

What might happen to your relationship when you watch or read the same story together?

_____

_____

_____

_____

_____

_____

_____

_____

_____

_____

_____

_____

_____

_____

_____

_____

_____

_____

_____

Tell a story. What are some personal or family stories you could share with your seventh grader to help shape their perspective about friendship, growing up, and personal values this year?

_____

_____

_____

_____

_____

_____

_____

_____

_____

_____

_____

_____

_____

_____

_____

_____

_____

_____

Live a story. When a seventh grader serves others, they learn about someone else's story. This is a great phase to find a place to serve others alongside your preteen. Where could you volunteer together on a regular basis?

_____

_____

_____

_____

_____

_____

_____

_____

_____

_____

_____

_____

_____

_____

_____

_____

_____

_____

EVERY KID

NEEDS

work

OVER TIME

—

TO GIVE

THEM

significance.

WORK YOUR SEVENTH GRADER CAN DO

DO HOMEWORK
INDEPENDENTLY

VACUUM THE
FAMILY VEHICLE

LOOK AFTER SIBLINGS

SORT, WASH, FOLD, AND
PUT AWAY LAUNDRY

DOWNLOAD AND
CLIP COUPONS

PREPARE A FAMILY MEAL

TAKE OUT THE
TRASH / RECYCLING

LEARN TO IRON CLOTHES

CHANGE LIGHT BULBS

MAKE A GROCERY LIST

USE A HANDSAW AND A
POCKETKNIFE

PRACTICE A SPORT,
MUSICAL INSTRUMENT,
OR OTHER SKILL

What are some ways your seventh grader already shows responsibility at home, at school, and in-between?

_____

_____

_____

_____

_____

_____

_____

_____

_____

_____

_____

_____

_____

_____

_____

_____

_____

_____

_____

_____

Your seventh grader may struggle with time management, so help them prioritize. Which of their responsibilities matter most to you and your family?

_____

_____

_____

_____

_____

_____

_____

_____

_____

_____

_____

_____

_____

_____

_____

_____

_____

_____

_____

Some days might be easier than others to motivate your seventh grader. What are some strategies you could employ to keep your seventh grader motivated?

_____

_____

_____

_____

_____

_____

_____

_____

_____

_____

_____

_____

_____

_____

_____

_____

_____

_____

_____

What are things you hope your seventh grader will be able to do independently in the next phase? How are you helping them develop those skills now?

EVERY KID

NEEDS

fun

OVER TIME

—

TO GIVE

THEM

connection.

WAYS TO HAVE FUN
WITH YOUR SEVENTH GRADER

BOARD GAMES:

CATCH PHRASE®	**BALDERDASH®**	**TABOO®**
APPLES TO APPLES®	**SAY ANYTHING®**	**RUMMIKUB®**

CARD GAMES:

SPOONS	**CRAZY EIGHTS**	**MONOPOLY DEAL**
SLAP JACK	**B.S. / I DOUBT IT**	**MAFIA**

ACTIVITIES:

ART CLASSES	**TASTE TEST** (pizza from 4 places in town—which is the best?)	**GLOW BOWLING** (blacklight bowling)
AN ESCAPE ROOM		**GLOW GOLF, MINI GOLF**
EVENTS AT THE LIBRARY	**FLY A KITE**	**ARCADE GAMES**
LOCAL MUSEUMS / THEATER	**LOCAL SPORTING EVENT**	**APP GAMES** (compete against each other)
LASER TAG	**SOCCER GOLF / SOCCER TENNIS**	**PHOTO SHOOT**
WATER PARK		
FAMILY NETFLIX® ROULETTE	**TRAIN FOR A 5K**	**GO KARTS**

What are some activities your seventh grader enjoys that you could do as a family (*and maybe sometimes include their friends*)?

_____

_____

_____

_____

_____

_____

_____

_____

_____

_____

_____

_____

_____

_____

_____

_____

_____

_____

What are some activities your seventh grader enjoys that you could occasionally do together, one-on-one?

_____

_____

_____

_____

_____

_____

_____

_____

When are the best times of the day, or week, for you to set aside to just have fun with your seventh grader?

_____

_____

_____

_____

_____

_____

_____

Some days are *extra* fun days. What are some ways you want to celebrate special days this year?

NEXT BIRTHDAY

_____

_____

_____

_____

_____

_____

_____

_____

_____

_____

_____

_____

_____

_____

_____

_____

HOLIDAYS

Consider celebrating a few random holidays: the first/last day
of school, Jelly Bean Day, No Socks Day.

EVERY KID

NEEDS

tribes

OVER TIME

—

TO GIVE

THEM

belonging.

ADULTS WHO MIGHT INFLUENCE YOUR SEVENTH GRADER

PARENTS

YOUTUBE & CULTURAL ICONS

SCHOOL WORKERS

GRANDPARENTS

FRIENDS' PARENTS

CHURCH LEADERS

AUNTS & UNCLES

SEVENTH GRADE TEACHERS

COACHES & CLUB LEADERS

You already know friends matter to your seventh grader, but it's easy to forget that seventh graders also need other adults in their tribe. List at least five adults who have the potential to positively influence your seventh grader.

_____

_____

_____

_____

_____

_____

_____

_____

_____

_____

_____

_____

_____

_____

_____

_____

_____

_____

_____

What is one thing these adults could do for your seventh grader this year?

_____

_____

_____

_____

_____

_____

_____

_____

_____

_____

_____

_____

_____

_____

_____

_____

_____

_____

_____

_____

What are a few ways you could show these adults appreciation
for the significant role they play in your kid's life?

_____

_____

_____

_____

_____

_____

_____

_____

_____

_____

_____

_____

_____

_____

_____

_____

_____

EVERY KID

NEEDS

words

OVER TIME

—

TO GIVE

THEM

direction.

WORDS YOUR SEVENTH GRADER NEEDS TO HEAR

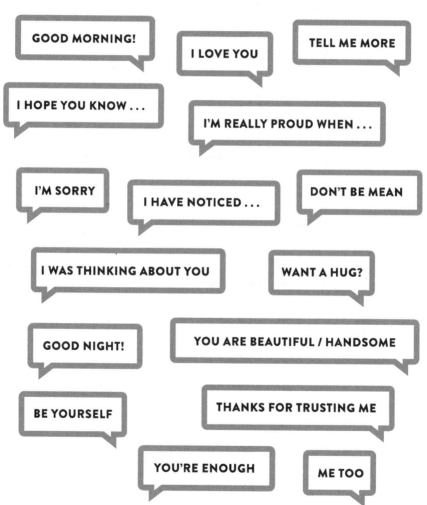

GOOD MORNING!

I LOVE YOU

TELL ME MORE

I HOPE YOU KNOW . . .

I'M REALLY PROUD WHEN . . .

I'M SORRY

I HAVE NOTICED . . .

DON'T BE MEAN

I WAS THINKING ABOUT YOU

WANT A HUG?

GOOD NIGHT!

YOU ARE BEAUTIFUL / HANDSOME

BE YOURSELF

THANKS FOR TRUSTING ME

YOU'RE ENOUGH

ME TOO

What are some ways you can share personal and specific encouragement with your seventh grader?

Hint: You might start with the things that impress you about your kid from page 27.

Many middle schoolers are inspired by words from a song lyric, quote, or Scripture. How can you discover the words that mean something to your middle schooler?

What are some quotes, lyrics, Scriptures, or inspirational thoughts you want to share with your sixth grader? How might you share those in a way that resonates with them?

_____

_____

_____

_____

_____

_____

_____

_____

_____

_____

_____

_____

_____

_____

_____

_____

_____

_____

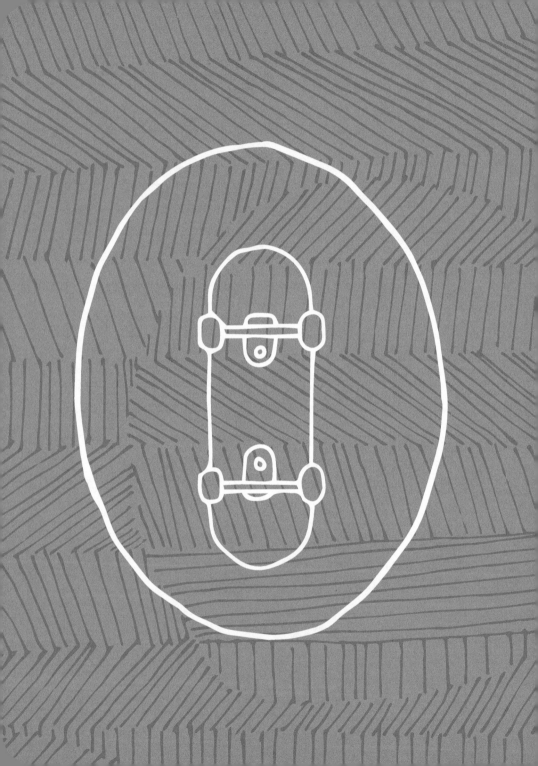

FOUR CONVERSATIONS

TO HAVE IN THIS PHASE

WHEN YOU KNOW
WHERE YOU WANT
TO GO,

AND YOU KNOW
WHERE YOU ARE
NOW,

YOU CAN ALWAYS
DO SOMETHING

TO MOVE IN A
BETTER DIRECTION.

OVER THE NEXT 312 WEEKS OF YOUR CHILD'S LIFE, SOME CONVERSATIONS MAY MATTER MORE THAN OTHERS.

WHAT YOU SAY, FOR EXAMPLE, REGARDING . . .
Music Genres
Clothing Brands
and Sports Teams

MIGHT HAVE LESS IMPACT ON THEIR FUTURE THAN WHAT YOU SAY REGARDING . . .
Health
Sex
Technology
or Faith.

The next pages are about the conversations that matter most. On the left page is a destination—what you might want to be true in your kid's life 312 weeks from now. On the right page is a goal for conversations with your seventh grader this year and a few suggestions about what you might want to say.

Healthy habits

—

LEARNING TO STRENGTHEN MY BODY THROUGH EXERCISE, NUTRITION, AND SELF-ADVOCACY

THIS YEAR YOU WILL

DEVELOP POSITIVE ROUTINES

SO YOUR SEVENTH GRADER WILL VALUE THEIR

CHANGING BODY AND MAINTAIN GOOD HYGIENE.

Some healthy habits happen without conversation—just by exercising and playing outside with your seventh grader, and scheduling a physical once per year. You can also improve your seventh grader's habits with a few simple words.

SAY THINGS LIKE . . .

"WHAT DO YOU KNOW ABOUT ANOREXIA/CUTTING/ PROTEIN SUPPLEMENTS?"
(Talk about body image.)

"WHAT ARE YOU LEARNING IN HEALTH CLASS?"
(Helping with a class project might be a great conversation starter.)

"LET'S DO THIS TOGETHER."
(Exercise or begin a healthy eating plan together.)

"WHAT WOULD YOU LIKE FOR DINNER THIS WEEK?"
(Let them participate in dinner plans, and eat together whenever possible.)

HOW CAN I HELP YOU FEEL LESS STRESSED?
(Help them regulate their emotional health.)

"TIME FOR BED!"
(Preteens need 10-11 hours of sleep.)

"SINCE YOU DIDN'T MAKE SOCCER, MAYBE YOU CAN TRY OUT FOR TRACK."
(Help put a failure into perspective.)

"WHEN WAS THE LAST TIME YOU DRANK SOME WATER?"
(Middle schoolers sometimes forget to stay hydrated when exercising—or when breathing.)

What are some activities you can do with your seventh grader that require a little bit of exercise?

_____

_____

_____

_____

_____

_____

_____

_____

_____

_____

_____

_____

_____

_____

_____

_____

_____

_____

Seventh graders can be sensitive about their bodies. What's one way you can promote a healthy body image for your seventh grader?

_____

_____

_____

_____

_____

_____

_____

_____

_____

_____

_____

_____

_____

_____

_____

_____

_____

Kids who cook learn what ingredients are in the things they eat. What are some simple ways your seventh grader can help you in the kitchen?

_____

_____

_____

_____

_____

_____

_____

_____

_____

_____

_____

_____

_____

_____

_____

_____

_____

_____

What are your own health goals for this year? How can you improve the habits in your own life?

_____

_____

_____

_____

_____

_____

_____

_____

_____

_____

_____

_____

_____

_____

_____

_____

_____

_____

Sexual integrity

—

GUARDING MY POTENTIAL FOR INTIMACY THROUGH APPROPRIATE BOUNDARIES AND MUTUAL RESPECT

THIS YEAR YOU WILL

INTERPRET WHAT IS CHANGING

SO YOUR SEVENTH GRADER WILL RESPECT THEMSELVES AND GROW IN CONFIDENCE.

Seventh graders are intensely curious about sex, dating, and their changing bodies. According to the American Academy of Pediatrics, on average, kids begin dating between 12-13 years old. So chances are pretty good that your seventh grader has at least *thought about* the idea of a romantic relationship. Let your seventh grader know you are a safe place to process their questions.

SAY THINGS LIKE . . .

WHO DO YOU KNOW THAT IS DATING?

"I LOVE THE WAY YOUR EYES SHINE WHEN YOU LAUGH."
(Increase positive affirmation and affection.)

WHAT DOES DATING MEAN?

"WHAT DOES IT MEAN TO HONOR GOD WITH YOUR BODY?"
(Help them personalize boundaries.)

"I'M HERE IF YOU WANT TO TALK."

"THAT'S A GOOD QUESTION. I'M SO GLAD YOU ASKED ME."
(Answer questions about sex in detail; if you don't, the Internet will.)

"THANK YOU FOR TALKING ABOUT THIS. CAN WE TALK ABOUT IT AGAIN ANOTHER TIME?"
(Always finish the conversation with room to pick it back up again later.)

When it comes to your kid's sexuality, what do you hope is true for them 312 weeks from now?

_____

_____

_____

_____

_____

_____

_____

_____

_____

_____

_____

_____

_____

_____

_____

_____

_____

_____

_____

What are the biggest points of tension with your seventh grader when it comes to modesty, sexual language, dating, peer pressure, or issues of sexual integrity? Who can you go to for advice on these issues?

_____

_____

_____

_____

_____

_____

_____

_____

_____

_____

_____

_____

_____

_____

_____

_____

_____

_____

_____

Be prepared. 22% of seventh graders report having sexted in the past six months. Pause. Breathe. Now, write down two or three things you want to say to your kid if you were to discover something you hadn't expected when it comes to their sexuality.

_____

_____

_____

_____

_____

_____

_____

_____

_____

_____

_____

_____

_____

_____

_____

_____

_____

_____

_____

When your seventh grader has questions they won't ask you, who do you hope they will go to for advice?

HINT: Whoever that person is, let them know. And let your seventh grader know.

_____

_____

_____

_____

_____

_____

_____

_____

_____

_____

_____

_____

_____

_____

_____

_____

_____

_____

Technological responsibility

—

LEVERAGING THE POTENTIAL OF ONLINE EXPERIENCES TO ENHANCE MY OFFLINE COMMUNITY AND SUCCESS

THIS YEAR YOU WILL

COLLABORATE A PLAN

SO YOUR SEVENTH GRADER WILL RESPECT LIMITS
AND STRENGTHEN SOCIAL ABILITIES

Your seventh grader is now a publisher. Whether the content they publish exists in a text thread or on the Internet, there are some important conversations to have with your seventh grader about how they use mobile devices and what kind of content they create.

SAY THINGS LIKE . . .

"LET ME CHECK THE AGE RESTRICTIONS FIRST."
(Most social platforms require a minimum age of 13 years.)

"SAW THIS VIDEO AND IT MADE ME THINK OF YOU."
(Use technology to connect throughout the day—with no agenda.)

"WE SHOULD RESPECT PEOPLE ONLINE AS MUCH AS WE RESPECT THEM IN PERSON."
(Talk about how devices sometimes escalate bullying.)

WHAT YOU POST IS PUBLIC, EVEN IF IT FEELS PRIVATE, AND IT CAN BE PERMANENT.
(Help them recognize potential risks related to the words, images, and videos they create.)

"I NEED YOUR PHONE AT 7 PM EVERY NIGHT."
(Whatever your expectations may be, make them clear up front.)

"CAN YOU TEACH ME HOW TO USE THIS APP?"
(Use mobile devices to connect: text, share, learn, and play together.)

When it comes to your kid's engagement with technology, what do you hope is true for them 312 weeks from now?

_____

_____

_____

_____

_____

_____

_____

_____

_____

_____

_____

_____

_____

_____

_____

_____

_____

_____

_____

What rules do you have for digital devices in your family? If you don't have any, what are two or three you might want to set for your seventh grader?

_____

_____

_____

_____

_____

_____

_____

_____

_____

_____

_____

_____

_____

_____

_____

_____

_____

_____

What are your own personal values and disciplines when it comes to leveraging technology? Are there ways you want to improve your own savvy, skill, or responsibility in this area?

_____

_____

_____

_____

_____

_____

_____

_____

_____

_____

_____

_____

_____

_____

_____

_____

_____

_____

LET'S TALK ABOUT SOCIAL MEDIA.

Your seventh grader is probably interested in opening an account, and you may be digging in your heels. Sometime when your seventh grader isn't around to pressure you, here are a few things to consider:

What are the pros and cons of allowing your seventh grader to open social media accounts?

_____

_____

_____

_____

_____

_____

_____

_____

_____

_____

_____

_____

_____

_____

When do you feel is the ideal age for your kid to open social media accounts?

_____

_____

_____

_____

_____

_____

_____

_____

What are some ways you want to monitor the content they view or publish to social media accounts in the beginning?

_____

_____

_____

_____

_____

_____

_____

How can you set expectations so your kid knows they can earn more freedom on social media platforms over time?

_____

_____

_____

_____

_____

_____

_____

_____

_____

_____

_____

_____

_____

_____

_____

_____

_____

_____

_____

_____

_____

_____

Authentic faith

—

**TRUSTING JESUS
IN A WAY THAT
TRANSFORMS HOW
I LOVE GOD,
MYSELF,
AND THE REST
OF THE WORLD**

THIS YEAR YOU WILL

PROVOKE DISCOVERY

SO YOUR SEVENTH GRADER WILL OWN THEIR OWN FAITH AND VALUE A FAITH COMMUNITY.

In this phase, your seventh grader may be asking some hard questions. Don't be shocked (at least not visibly). Doubt isn't toxic to your middle schooler's faith; it's part of the process of personalizing what they believe. Make your home a safe place for them to ask questions, and show interest in what they are learning.

SAY THINGS LIKE . . .

WHEN DO YOU FEEL CLOSEST TO GOD?

"IN THIS WORLD YOU WILL HAVE TROUBLE. BUT TAKE HEART! I HAVE OVERCOME THE WORLD." John 16:33 (Repeat simple Bible verses.)

"CAN WE PRAY ABOUT THIS TOGETHER?"

"HOW CAN I PRAY FOR YOU TODAY / THIS WEEK?"

"GOD MADE YOU, HE KNOWS YOU, AND HE LOVES YOU."

"THE WAY YOU LIVE CAN SHOW OTHERS WHO JESUS IS."

"WHAT WOULD BE A FUN WAY WE COULD SERVE OTHERS TOGETHER?" (Consider serving at your church or a local ministry that appeals to your seventh grader's interests.)

"THAT'S A GREAT QUESTION. I DON'T KNOW THE ANSWER, BUT WE CAN FIND OUT."

"I HAVE QUESTIONS, TOO. WHAT OTHER THINGS DO YOU WONDER ABOUT?"

"I DON'T KNOW WHY . . . BUT I DO KNOW GOD IS GOOD."

What are some ways you can help deepen your seventh grader's connection with friends who follow Jesus?

_____

_____

_____

_____

_____

_____

_____

_____

_____

_____

_____

_____

_____

_____

_____

_____

_____

_____

_____

_____

_____

What are some ways you can help deepen your seventh grader's connection with adults whose faith they admire?

_____

_____

_____

_____

_____

_____

_____

_____

_____

_____

_____

_____

_____

_____

_____

_____

_____

_____

_____

What are some overnight or weekend opportunities provided by your church or a local youth ministry? (*Over the next 312 weeks, prioritize these experiences. Put the dates on the calendar early. Allow them to invite a friend if they are nervous to go "alone." Look for scholarships or help your kid raise money.*)

_____

_____

_____

_____

_____

_____

_____

_____

_____

_____

_____

_____

_____

_____

_____

What routines or habits do you have in your own life that are stretching your faith?

_____

_____

_____

_____

_____

_____

_____

_____

_____

_____

_____

_____

_____

_____

_____

_____

_____

_____

_____

THE

rhythm

OF YOUR

WEEK

—

WILL SHAPE

THE VALUES

IN YOUR

home.

NOW THAT YOU HAVE FILLED THIS BOOK WITH IDEAS AND GOALS, IT MAY SEEM AS IF YOU WILL NEVER HAVE TIME TO GET IT ALL DONE.

Actually, you have *312 weeks.*

And every week has potential.

The secret to making the most of this phase is to take advantage of the time you already have. On average, you probably spend around four hours each day with your middle schooler. (In high school that number will drop in half.) So, make the most of these four times together.

Instill purpose by starting the day with encouraging words.

Interpret life during informal conversations as you travel.

Establish values with intentional conversations while you eat together.

Listen to their heart by staying available—just in case.

How are you adjusting to a new rhythm in this phase?

What are some of your favorite routines with your seventh grader?

Write down any other thoughts or questions about parenting your seventh grader.

TO LOVE GOD

Provoke
discovery

→

SO THEY WILL . . .
TRUST GOD'S CHARACTER
& EXPERIENCE GOD'S FAMILY

WISDOM
(First day of school)

FAITH
(Trust Jesus)

AY?

DO I HAVE YOUR ATTENTION?	**DO I HAVE WHAT IT TAKES?**	**DO I HAVE FRIENDS?**
K & FIRST	SECOND & THIRD	FOURTH & FIFTH

ENGAGE their interests

EVERY KID $\longrightarrow$ MADE I
THE IMA
OF GO

Incite
wonder $\longrightarrow$ SO THEY WILL . . .
KNOW GOD'S LOVE
& MEET GOD'S FAMILY

BEGINNING
(Baby dedication)

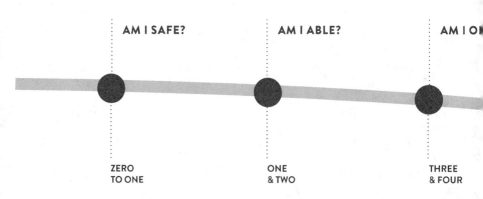

AM I SAFE?   AM I ABLE?   AM I O

ZERO
TO ONE   ONE
& TWO   THREE
& FOUR

EMBRACE *their physical needs*

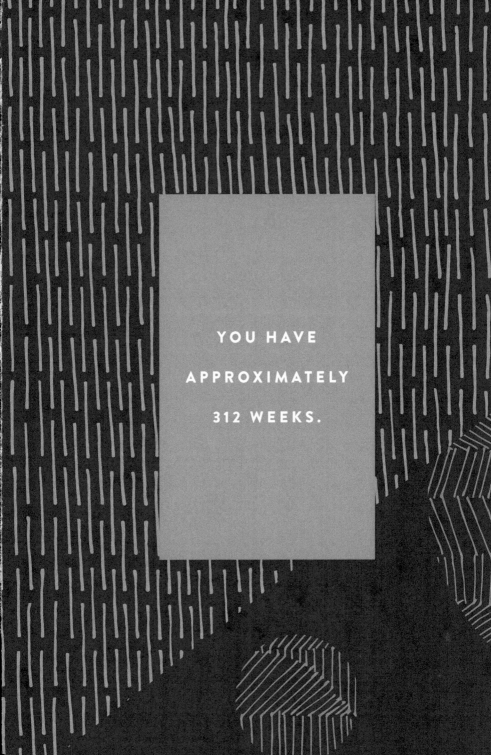

YOU HAVE

APPROXIMATELY

312 WEEKS.

IT'S JUST
A PHASE
SO DON'T
MISS IT.

ND

trust Jesus →

TO HAVE A BETTER FUTURE

Fuel

passion

→

SO THEY WILL . . .
KEEP PURSUING AUTHENTIC FAITH
& DISCOVER A PERSONAL MISSION

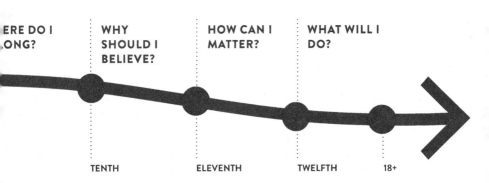

FREEDOM
(Driver's license)

GRADUATION
(Moving on)

ERE DO I
ONG?

WHY SHOULD I BELIEVE?

HOW CAN I MATTER?

WHAT WILL I DO?

TENTH   ELEVENTH   TWELFTH   18+

MOBILIZE their potential

WITH
ALL THEIR

HEART

SOUL

STRENGTH

A

Provoke
discovery → SO THEY WILL . . .
OWN THEIR OWN FAITH
& VALUE A FAITH COMMUNITY

IDENTITY
(Coming of age)

WHO DO I LIKE?   WHO AM I?   WHO DO I
WANT TO BE?   WH
BE

SIXTH   SEVENTH   EIGHTH   NINTH

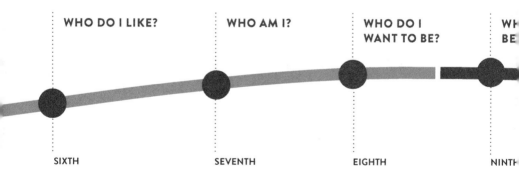

AFFIRM **their personal journey**

ABOUT THE AUTHORS

KRISTEN IVY @kristen_ivy

Kristen Ivy is executive director of the Phase Project. She and her husband, Matt, are in the preschool and elementary phases with three kids: Sawyer, Hensley, and Raleigh.

Kristen earned her Bachelors of Education from Baylor University in 2004 and received a Master of Divinity from Mercer University in 2009. She worked in the public school system as a high school biology and English teacher, where she learned firsthand the importance of influencing the next generation.

Kristen is also the executive director of messaging at Orange and has played an integral role in the development of the elementary, middle school, and high school curriculum and has shared her experiences at speaking events across the country. She is the co-author of *Playing for Keeps, Creating a Lead Small Culture, It's Just a Phase*, and *Don't Miss It*.

REGGIE JOINER @reggiejoiner

Reggie Joiner is founder and CEO of the reThink Group and co-founder of the Phase Project. He and his wife, Debbie, have reared four kids into adulthood. They now also have two grandchildren.

The reThink Group (also known as Orange) is a non-profit organization whose purpose is to influence those who influence the next generation. Orange provides resources and training for churches and organizations that create environments for parents, kids, and teenagers.

Before starting the reThink Group in 2006, Reggie was one of the founders of North Point Community Church. During his 11 years with Andy Stanley, Reggie was the executive director of family ministry, where he developed a new concept for relevant ministry to children, teenagers, and married adults. Reggie has authored and co-authored more than 10 books including: *Think Orange, Seven Practices of Effective Ministry, Parenting Beyond Your Capacity, Playing for Keeps, Lead Small, Creating a Lead Small Culture,* and his latest, *A New Kind of Leader* and *Don't Miss It.*

MAKE THE MOST OF EVERY PHASE IN YOUR CHILD'S LIFE

The guide in your hand is one of an eighteen-part series.

So, unless you've figured out a way to freeze time and keep your seventh grader from turning into a eighth grader, you might want to check out the next guide in this set.

Designed in partnership with Parent Cue, each guide will help you rediscover . . .

what's changing about your kid,
the 6 things your kid needs most,
and 4 conversations to have each year.

WANT TO GIFT A FRIEND WITH ALL 18 GUIDES
OR HAVE ALL THE GUIDES ON HAND FOR YOURSELF?

ORDER THE ENTIRE SERIES OF PHASE GUIDES TODAY.

ORDER NOW AT: **WWW.PHASEGUIDES.COM**